Furry Logic

For Mark and Sabine

10TH ANNIVERSARY EDITION

Furry Logic

A Guide to Life's Little Challenges

Jane Seabrook

TEN SPEED PRESS
Berkeley

Smile

first thing

in the morning.

Get it over with.

I would be unstoppable.

If I could just get started.

It might look like I'm doing nothing,

but at the cellular level I'm really

quite busy.

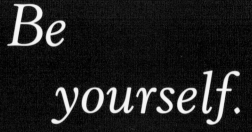

Nobody

is

better

qualified.

Life is

full of challenge

and frustration.

But sooner or later

you'll find the

hairstyle you like.

Delusions of grandeur

make me feel a lot better about myself.

Always remember you are unique . . .

just like everyone else.

If at first

you do succeed,

try not to look

too astonished.

If at first

you don't succeed,

swallow all evidence

that you tried.

No one is listening

until you make a mistake.

Wake me up

when everything is organized.

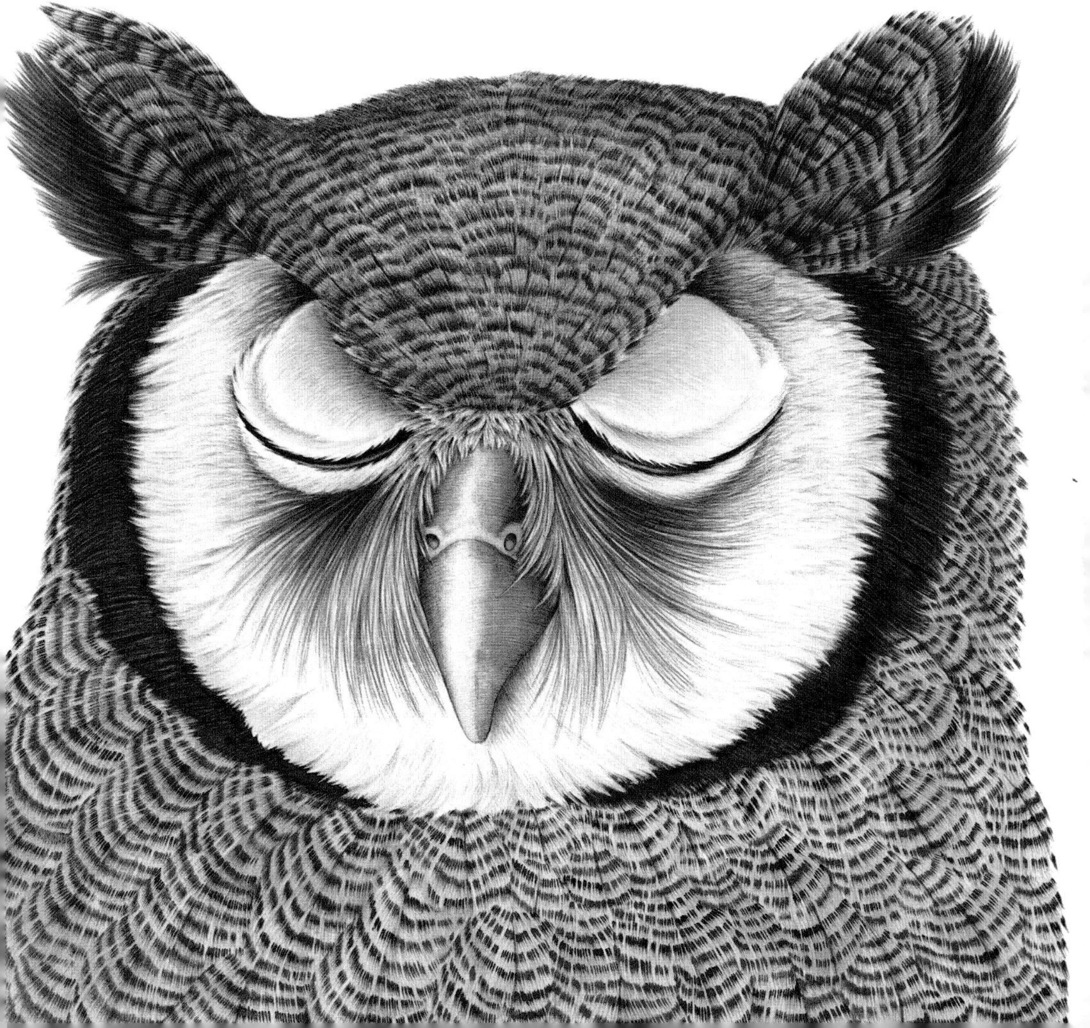

Consciousness:
that annoying time between naps.

I never made

Who's Who

but I'm featured in

What's That.

All power corrupts.

Absolute power is kinda neat.

The

trouble

with work

is . . .

it's

so

daily.

I hear the call to do nothing,

and am doing my best

to answer it.

I try to take

one day at a time . . .

but

sometimes

several days

attack me

at once.

I am not *tense.*

Just terribly, terribly alert.

When you're in it up to your ears . . .

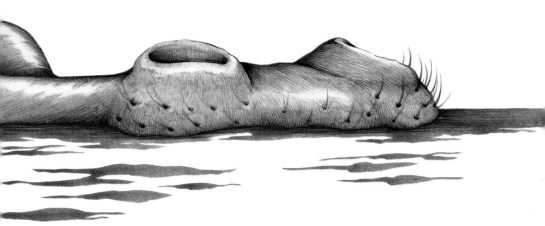

it pays to keep your mouth shut.

If you can keep

your head when

all those around you

are losing theirs—

it's quite possible

you haven't grasped

the situation.

I have one nerve left,

and you're getting on it.

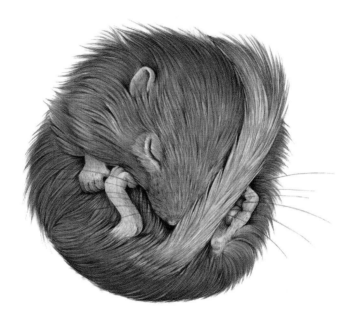

No day is so bad

that it can't be fixed

with a nap.

By doing just a little every day,

I can gradually let the task

completely overwhelm me.

If you don't agree with me,

it means . . .

you haven't been listening.

You don't have to

agree with me,

but it's quicker.

Never go to bed mad—

stay up and fight.

You'll always be my best friend . . .

you

know

too

much.

Your secrets are safe with me . . .

and all my friends.

I don't repeat gossip.

So listen carefully.

Do

you

believe

in love

at first

sight?

Or

should

I walk

past

again?

Anyone can be passionate.

But it takes real lovers to be silly.

Too much of a good thing

can be wonderful.

If you leave me . . .

can I come too?

The moment

you have children,

you forgive

your parents . . .

everything.

Please don't tell me to relax—

it's only my tension that's

holding me together.

The

quickest

way for

a parent

to get a

child's

attention . . .

is

to

sit

down

and

look

comfortable.

There are few things more satisfying

than seeing your children

have teenagers of their own.

You can't stay

young forever.

But you

can be

immature

for the

rest of your life.

I want it all—

and I want it delivered!

I didn't claw my way

to the top of the food chain

to eat roughage!

Never eat more

than you can lift.

I'm on the brink of happiness—

will you give me a push?

It's been lovely.

But I have to s c r e a m now.

Artist's Notes

I have enjoyed every minute of creating
the characters that make up *Furry Logic,*
and to think that all this fun has lasted ten
years is truly unbelievable. The anniversary book
is the ninth in the series and a chance for me to reflect
on how it began—with some of the first paintings that appear in this book—
and grew to a collection that is now several hundred in number and that has
found homes all around the world.

All the paintings are watercolor, my favorite medium—mainly because I've
never been brave enough to try oils! The wonderful thing about watercolor is
just how versatile it is, from a translucent single layer to rich and deep color
built up layer upon layer with a dry brush. The layering, of course, is just perfect

for fur or feathers: light and shade. I achieve the detail
in my paintings with a very fine sable brush, a single hair
at its tip. The single hair inevitably wears out by the end
of each painting, sometimes partway through. Most of
the expression in the animals I paint is to be found
in the eyes, so that is where I start—the whites of the eyes
often lending the intensity when a quote calls for it!

Thank you to everyone who has been in touch over the years to say they have enjoyed the books. It's great that so many PowerPoint presentations have been punctuated with *Furry Logic*, and I love all the other imaginative ways it has been used, from hand-sewn quilts to an exquisitely embroidered "I am *not* tense. Just terribly, terribly alert" meerkat.

I hope you have enjoyed the anniversary selection, and I always appreciate receiving your comments and suggestions via the website at furrylogic.com.

Best wishes

Jane

Acknowledgments

Heartfelt thanks to Mark Seabrook-Davison, Burton Silver, and Mark Seabrook, whom *Furry Logic* depended upon in different ways for its start in the world.

Thank you to the people at Image Centre, especially Troy Caltaux and Alex Trimbach, and to Aaron Wehner and Lisa Westmoreland at Ten Speed Press for their support and encouragement.

Thanks to Ashleigh Brilliant for permission to reproduce the following quotations that appear in the book: "I'm on the brink of happiness—will you give me a push?" "Wake me up when everything is organized." "By doing just a little every day, I can gradually let the task completely overwhelm me." "Please don't tell me to relax—it's only my tension that's holding me together." "I hear the call to do nothing, and am doing my best to answer it." "I try to take one day at a time . . . but sometimes several days attack me at once." These quotations are from the Ashleigh Brilliant Pot-Shot series. For more information, visit www.ashleighbrilliant.com.

Grateful thanks to John Cooney of *Grapevine* magazine, Auckland, New Zealand, for sharing many of the quotations attributed to "Anon."

Other quotations appeared or are quoted in the following publications: "Be yourself. Nobody is better qualified." (Anon.) in *More Pocket Positives*, Five Mile Press, Melbourne, Australia; "If at first you do succeed, try not to look too astonished." (Anon.) in *World's Best Humour*, Five Mile Press, Melbourne, Australia; "I never made Who's Who but I'm featured in What's That." (Phyllis Diller), "Never go to bed mad—stay up and fight." (Phyllis Diller), and "You can't stay young forever. But you can be immature for the rest of your life." (Maxine Wilkie) in *Women's Lip*, ed. Roz Warren, Sourcebooks Inc., USA; "If you don't agree with me, it means you haven't been listening." (Sam Markewich) in *Comedy Comes Clean 2*, Three Rivers Press, NY, USA; "If you leave me, can I come too?" (Cynthia Hemmel) in *The Penguin Dictionary of Modern Humorous Quotations*, ed. Fred Metcalf, Penguin Group, UK; "Delusions of grandeur make me feel a lot better about myself" (Jane Wagner) in *The 637 Best Things Anyone Ever Said*, Robert Byrne, Ballantine Books, UK. Thank you also to readers who sent in quotes.

Published in the United States by Ten Speed Press, an imprint of the Crown Publishing Group,
a division of Random House LLC, a Penguin Random House Company, New York.
www.crownpublishing.com
www.tenspeed.com

Ten Speed Press and the Ten Speed Press colophon are registered trademarks of Random House LLC.

Originally published in the United States in somewhat different form by Ten Speed Press, Berkeley,
in 2004. Some material in this collection was first published by Ten Speed Press, Berkeley, as part of
Furry Logic: Wild Wisdom, *Purry Logic*, and *Furry Logic: Love*, in 2007, 2008, and 2010, respectively.

Library of Congress Cataloging-in-Publication Data
Seabrook, Jane.
  Furry logic, 10th anniversary edition : a guide to life's little challenges / Jane Seabrook.
      pages cm
   Summary: "A collection of adorable watercolor illustrations of animals paired with humorous
sayings about life and its little challenges"—Provided by publisher.
1. Conduct of life—Humor. 2. Animals—Pictorial works. I. Title.
  PN6231.C6142S4265 2014
  818'.602—dc23

2014014082

Hardcover ISBN: 978-1-60774-716-1
eBook ISBN: 978-1-60774-717-8

Printed in China

Design by Chloe Rawlins

10 9 8 7 6 5

Tenth Anniversary Edition